Tom Sherrington

ROSENSHINE'S PRINCIPLES IN ACTION

with illustrations by Oliver Caviglioli

First Published 2019

by John Catt Educational Ltd,
15 Riduna Park, Station Road,
Melton, Woodbridge IP12 1QT

Tel: +44 (0) 1394 389850
Email: enquiries@johncatt.com
Website: www.johncatt.com

Opinions expressed in this publication are those
of the contributors and are not necessarily those
of the publishers or the editors. We cannot accept
responsibility for any errors or omissions.

ISBN: 978 1 912906 20 8

Set and designed by John Catt Educational Limited

TABLE OF CONTENTS

INTRODUCTION: WHY ARE BARAK ROSENSHINE'S 'PRINCIPLES OF INSTRUCTION' SO GOOD?

I first encountered Barak Rosenshine's 'Principles of Instruction' after the British educator and graphic illustrator Oliver Caviglioli shared his excellent visual guide on Twitter. This prompted me to seek out the *American Educator* article from 2012 where Rosenshine's ideas are set out. This article is taken almost directly from a pamphlet in the International Academy of Education (IAE) *Educational Practices* series in 2010. In his pamphlet Rosenshine set out ten research-based principles of instruction based on the ideas he and his colleagues had developed over the preceding decades.

On first reading, I was struck immediately by its brilliant clarity and simplicity and its potential to support teachers seeking to engage with cognitive science and the wider world of education research. In the last year, Rosenshine's 'Principles of Instruction' has been circulating increasingly rapidly around schools in the UK as more teachers discover its insights, sharing via social media and the growing array of grassroots teacher conferences.

The purpose of writing this short booklet is to capture some of the many discussions I've had with school leaders and teachers, taking the ideas off the page and putting them into action in the classroom. Although the principles are superbly helpful as Rosenshine has expressed them, my hope is that this booklet provides an extra layer of guidance that people find interesting and useful, informing their staff training programmes or the development of their personal practice.

Four strands

The organisation of ideas that make up 'Principles of Instruction' has evolved over time. In 'Teaching Functions', 1986, there were six main ideas. In the IAE pamphlet, Rosenshine outlines 17 'instructional procedures' that emerge from the research:

- Begin a lesson with a short review of previous learning.

- Present new material in small steps with student practice after each step.

- Limit the amount of material students receive at one time.

- Give clear and detailed instructions and explanations.

- Ask a large number of questions and check for understanding.

- Provide a high level of active practice for all students.

- Guide students as they begin to practice.

- Think aloud and model steps.

- Provide models of worked-out problems.

- Ask students to explain what they had learned.

- Check the responses of all students.

- Provide systematic feedback and corrections.

- Use more time to provide explanations.

- Provide many examples.

- Re-teach material when necessary.

- Prepare students for independent practice.

- Monitor students when they begin independent practice.

From these procedures he then formulates the ten principles. In seeking to explain the principles to audiences in the UK during various ResearchEd[1] conferences, I found that it helps to condense these ten ideas down to four strands. Partly this is because of the requirements of timing a conference presentation where ten ideas feels like a long list. However, I mainly found that after revisiting the document many times, I was continually skipping back and forth to make these connections.

---

1   ResearchEd – A UK-based organisation running teacher conferences that focus on educational research and its implications for teachers and school leaders. www.researched.org.uk

The Principles of Instruction

1. Daily review.

2. Present new material using small steps.

3. Ask questions.

4. Provide models.

5. Guide student practice.

6. Check for student understanding.

7. Obtain a high success rate.

8. Provide scaffolds for difficult tasks.

9. Independent practice.

10. Weekly and monthly review.

Four strands

Sequencing concepts and modelling
2. Present new material using small steps.
4. Provide models.
8. Provide scaffolds for difficult tasks.

Questioning
3. Ask questions.
6. Check for student understanding.

Reviewing material
1. Daily review.
10. Weekly and monthly review.

Stages of practice
5. Guide student practice.
7. Obtain a high success rate.
9. Independent practice.

I will use the four strands structure for the guidance that follows. But first, I'd like to explore why the 'Principles of Instruction' pamphlet is receiving such an enthusiastic response. There are several reasons:

Bridging the research-practice divide

Rosenshine provides a highly accessible bridge between research and classroom practice. His principles are short, easy to read, and packed with insights. This is refreshing. From a teacher's perspective, research is still hard to access. A lot of original research languishes in obscure journals that most teachers don't even know exist. Even when wonderful communicators like Daniel Willingham, John Hattie, Dylan Wiliam – or, more recently, Efrat Furst, Yana Weinstein and Megan Sumeracki (members of The Learning Scientists) – publish books and blogs, it is still a challenge to secure major engagement across a large group of staff in a school. This is partly due to the limitations of teachers' time – they are busy! – but it's also a matter of school culture. Schools carry a lot of inertia; teachers' habits are hard to shift. The punchy simplicity of the principles cuts through a lot of that.

In the original publication, each short section outlining one of the ten principles follows a clear and persuasive structure: 'Research findings' followed by 'In the classroom'. Rosenshine does a superb job of relating research findings to classroom practice in such a way that conveys the key outcome of the research without getting bogged down in methodology and problematic considerations of effect size. The 2010 paper carries all the citations for anyone wishing to look a little deeper. There's power in the simple binary descriptor Rosenshine deploys to get his message across: *more effective* teachers vs *less effective* teachers. We all understand that implicitly there's a sliding scale – that more layers of nuance lie beneath – but 'more effective' cuts to the chase. And who doesn't want to be in that camp!

Trustworthiness

In addition to highlighting samples of evidence, the overall tone and content of the principles give teachers confidence that these ideas are not fads; they are rooted in evidence that has stood the test of time. Rosenshine introduces his pamphlet with a brief overview of the three sources of evidence that have informed his principles:

- Research on how our brain acquires and uses new information: *cognitive science*
- Research on the common classroom practices of those teachers whose students show the highest gains: *observational studies of 'master teachers'*
- Findings from studies that taught learning strategies to students: *testing cognitive supports and scaffolds that help students learn complex tasks*

He follows up with the acknowledgement that although the approaches are very different, 'there is no conflict at all between the instructional suggestions that come from each of these three sources. In other words, these three sources supplement and complement each other.' This fact 'gives us faith in the validity of these findings'.

The convergence of ideas from classroom observations and cognitive science is important. If it were the case that cognitive science suggested a different set of instructional practices from those being used by effective 'master' teachers, then we'd be in a muddle. How could we explain that? Happily, whilst learning and teaching are undeniably complex, it turns out that they are not *that* complex: we can formulate a coherent evidence-based model that links theory to practice. Rosenshine's Principles provide the coherence teachers seek, and that fosters trust. This matters because without trust, teachers don't buy into information; they simply ignore it, and the inertia grows.

Authenticity

A third aspect that I find to be fuelling interest in Rosenshine's 'Principles of Instruction' is that the paper, taken as whole, sounds to many teachers like common sense. It's an entirely recognisable set of ideas. There are no gimmicks, no fads, nothing that seems implausible, nothing outlandish. Teachers either recognise themselves in the descriptions or they see valid and obtainable models to aspire to. After many years of having teaching defined by external powers, this feels like a grassroots document, allowing it to gain acceptance that cuts through teachers' well-honed defence systems.

From my perspective, as someone who now spends most weeks working with teachers seeking to improve their practice, it's great to have a set of ideas that are rooted so authentically in classroom experience. This paper is uncontentious. The discussions are not about whether or not to adopt the principles; they are about how to adopt them more fluently, with more intensity or at a higher frequency; they are about how to interpret them through the lens of each subject domain, and how to adapt them for learners with different levels of knowledge and confidence.

For all these reasons, Barak Rosenshine's Principles of Instruction provide an incredibly useful platform for teacher development processes. It's a well-rehearsed notion that the lessons that make the difference to student outcomes are all the many lessons that go unobserved – where it is just the teacher and their students in a classroom enacting the teacher-student interactions that either lead to learning gains or don't. If teachers are going to be successful in improving their practice, they have to be working consciously and deliberately to do so. Teachers need to be working on developing better habits, seeking to be more effective day in, day out when nobody else except their students is looking. The kiss of death to teacher development is a school culture or accountability framework that motivates 'speed camera' behaviours – where teachers turn on the style when they are under scrutiny only to revert to less effective practices the rest of the time. If we're to avoid that, then we've got to foster a professional culture where good ideas gain acceptance, credibility, and momentum. I find that in Rosenshine we have a superb tool for doing just that.

Theory of action: what is the underlying model?

One of the big variables I find in working with teachers in a range of contexts is their ideas about how learning works. How do the actions and activities that a teacher engages in – or that they require their students to engage in – lead to learning? Sometimes teachers talk in terms of concepts 'sinking in', and I often hear complaints that despite explaining a concept over and over, students still managed to misunderstand it – or even worse, despite seeming to have been successful in a lesson, they forgot it all immediately afterwards. Too many teachers still believe that teaching according to students' preferred learning styles is a good idea, even though this has been soundly debunked.[2]

All of these problems stem from a weak model of the learning process. If teachers are going to improve their practice, then it's essential for the ideas they are basing their thinking around to be formulated on a sound model. Understanding the model isn't a necessary condition for successfully implementing the strategies the model suggests, but my personal view is that teachers are more likely to connect with ideas and implement them well if they can formulate a mental model of learning that underpins the practice. This is supported by the work of Deans for Impact in their excellent *Practice with Purpose* document:

> Deliberate practice both produces and relies on mental models and mental representations to guide decisions. These models allow practitioners to self-monitor performance to improve their performance.[3]

It's fascinating to me just how well the Principles of Instruction are supported by the learning model that emerges from contemporary cognitive science. For the purposes of this short book, it will help to rehearse the key elements of this model. It is based on ideas from the following sources:

- Daniel T. Willingham's *Why Don't Students Like School?*

- Graham Nuthall's *The Hidden Lives of Learners*

- Arthur Shimamura's *MARGE: A Whole-Brain Learning Approach*

- Yana Weinstein and Megan Sumeracki's *Understanding How We Learn*

- The many others who collectively contribute to our understanding: Robert and Elizabeth Bjork, John Sweller, Paul Kirschner, Carol Dweck

A simple model for how memory works is based on the concept of building schemata in our long-term memory, as follows:

---

2   Sumeracki, M. and Weinstein, Y. with Caviglioli, O. (2018) *Understanding how we learn – a Visual Guide* Routledge.

3   Deans for Impact www.deansforimpact.org/resources/practice-with-purpose

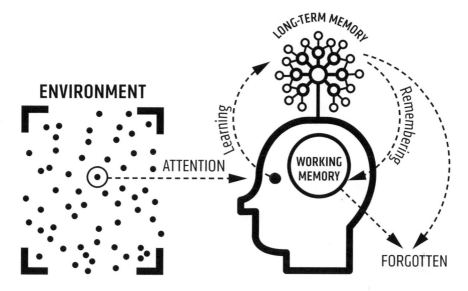

Conceptual information initially enters from the environment into our working memory.

Working memory is finite and actually rather small, so we can only absorb a limited amount of information at once.

We process information so that it is stored in our long-term memory. This is effectively unlimited, and we retrieve information back into our working memory as needed.

We organise information into schemata. Typically, new information is only stored if we can connect it to knowledge that we already have. As a result, prior knowledge is a major factor in our capacity to learn new information. The more complex and interconnected our schemata are, the easier it is to make sense of new related information and the better we are able to organise it so that it makes sense. The concept of understanding is really 'memory in disguise'.[4] This means that our schemata are more fully formed, are more interconnected, and can be explored and recalled more fluently.

If a schema contains incorrect information – a misconception or an incomplete model of how a process works – we can't simply overwrite it. A more primitive schema can return to dominate unless we unpick and fully re-learn a correct schema.

---

4   Willingham, D. (2009) *Why don't students like school?* Jossey-Bass

We forget information that we do not initially store successfully in a meaningful schema or that we do not retrieve frequently enough. This is entirely natural – we're primed to filter out information we might need and to discard the rest. Our capacity to retrieve information improves if we practise doing this more often and do so in more depth.

If we undertake enough retrieval practice, generating formulations of our memory and evaluating it for accuracy, we gain a degree of fluency and, ultimately, automaticity. This is true of anything we learn, be it reading, driving, or speaking a foreign language. A consequence of this, as explained by cognitive load theory,[5] is that the more fluent we are with retrieval of stored information, the more capacity we have in our working memory to attend to new information and problem-solving – if we are efficient in bringing up the information from memory, then there's more working memory space left to deal with applying the information. The opposite is also true: when we are less fluent with recall, our capacity to attend to new information and problem-solving is diminished. This is a key difference between novice and expert learners. Think of novice drivers, who become easily overwhelmed by the pressures of traffic and road signs: they are more likely to have difficulty absorbing all the external information as well as focusing on the skill of driving itself.

A key implication of this is that novice learners need more practice than more confident, experienced learners.

Following the work of Nuthall and Shimamura, I find it instructive to imagine a classroom of students as a room full of hidden schema-forming brains, each doing things we cannot see, each processing information differently depending on what they already know, on the level of attention they are giving to the new knowledge and on their capacity to self-regulate and to organise information successfully. In that context, instructional teaching needs to be highly interactive. We need to gain as much feedback as we can from our students, helping us gauge how well the learning is going so that we can then plan the next steps in our teaching. Learning is hidden, so we need to seek out evidence for it in a dynamic fashion during our lessons.

This interactivity, the need for 'responsive teaching'[6] underpins many of the ideas in the Principles of Instruction.

Knowledge-specified curriculum

A final preliminary consideration for teachers before we explore the principles themselves is the notion of a knowledge-specified or 'structured' curriculum.

5   Sweller, J., Ayres. P., Kalyuga, S. (2011) *Cognitive Load Theory* Springer
6   Wiliam, D. (2011) *Embedded Formative Assessment* Solution Tree Press

In the 1986 paper by Rosenshine and Stevens, 'Teaching Functions', they talk about the limitations of the principles:

> It would be a mistake to claim that the teaching procedures which have emerged from this research apply to all subjects, and all learners, all the time. Rather, these procedures are most applicable for the 'well-structured' (Simon, 1973) parts of any content area, and are least applicable to the 'ill-structured' parts of any content area.

They go on to explain that all subjects have 'well-structured' elements – some more than others. It's an important bit of nuance in the implementation of Rosenshine's principles. Evidently, some content needs more teacher-directed instruction and so the subject-specific curriculum context is important.

This also suggests that the more precise we are about the knowledge goals for learners, the more rigorous we can be about the process of ensuring that all students meet them. This rings true in my experience, having observed thousands of lessons. Very often, when engaging in feedback conversations with teachers, I feel that everyone in the class could have benefited from more precise knowledge goals – both teacher and students. It's hard to form a strong schema, to practice retrieval, or to evaluate the true extent of our knowledge if you are unsure what the knowledge is meant to be or if you are unsure what exactly 'success' looks like.

This will be illustrated further as we explore each of the principles.

In the following sections, I will take each strand in turn, referencing the original 17 instructional procedures where I think they belong. My aim is to amplify and augment the ideas as Rosenshine has expressed them, giving further examples without repeating those he used himself.

STRAND 1:
SEQUENCING CONCEPTS AND MODELLING

I've started here because it seems sensible to begin with elements of instruction that require advanced planning before we get into the classroom.

Relevant instructional procedures include:

- Present new material in small steps with student practice after each step.
- Limit the amount of material students receive at one time
- Give clear and detailed instructions and explanations.
- Think aloud and model steps.
- Use more time to provide explanations.
- Provide many examples.
- Re-teach material when necessary.

2. Present new material using small steps

Rosenshine suggests that more effective teachers recognise the need to deal with the limitations of working memory and succeed in breaking down concepts and procedures into small steps. They then ensure students have the opportunity to practise each of the steps. The modelling and scaffolding that accompany this phase of a lesson all roll into one as part of the process of explaining, providing well-structured support for students as they build their schemata for new concepts.

Clearly, the implication here is that teachers need to invest time in analysing their curriculum material to see how it can be broken down. We can't separate generic instructional methods from curriculum content in practice.

There are many examples of where material is broken down into small steps. It's a common idea in teaching sports where complex actions and team games are built around the development of specific definable skills. In dancing, we don't try to learn a whole routine from start to finish; we learn the first step and then the second, rehearsing each one. Then we add a third and fourth and maybe practise steps one to four before adding step five. We build slowly, seeking to secure success at each point whilst also assimilating each part into the whole.

Practise all the steps

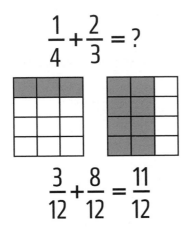

$$\frac{1}{4} + \frac{2}{3} = ?$$

$$\frac{3}{12} + \frac{8}{12} = \frac{11}{12}$$

1 Model for each fraction. What does each mean?

2 Terminology: numerator, denominator

3 Which fractions can we add directly?

4 Concept of multiples, finding lowest common multiples

5 Finding a common denominator

6 Scaling up numerator to keep fraction same size

7 Adding fractions with same denominator

8 Check against the shape model

Many mathematical procedures are similar. As shown above, adding fractions, broken down, actually comprises several steps.

A student who struggles to add fractions may need more practice with building a concrete model of fractions as parts of shapes or may need practice finding lowest common multiples.

There are many more examples, each of which is highly subject specific. I would argue that a great deal of teacher development time would be wisely spent analysing the curriculum, so that teachers have a clear understanding of what the learning steps might look like. Sometimes this is hard because of the 'curse of knowledge' that experts experience: we don't always know what we know; we accumulate a great deal of tacit knowledge from experience in our specialist areas and it requires some thought to map this out for our novice learners.

One common strand of thinking about new material is to break a task down into a set of instructions. How do you build a wall and, in doing so, how do you go about checking that it will be 100% straight and vertical in every plane as you go along? How do you bake a cake, from selecting and measuring the ingredients to knowing what 'the right consistency' of the mixture means? How do you construct a paragraph with a particular goal in mind, selecting words and phrases to convey the meaning, create the mood, and express the style that you want? How do you explain how diffusion of gases works, linking the physical reality to a model that helps explain what you see (or smell!), step by step? How do you deconstruct the process of composition in art? If teachers in the relevant discipline can break these complex activities down into fine-grained stages, they'll be more effective in explaining them to their students.

Another form of sequencing is in moving from the big picture of a subject down to a detailed area of focus and back again. We zoom out to orientate ourselves and then zoom in, ever further, step by step. This helps students to form a clear schema, locating an area of learning in relation to others. For example, each event in history has a wider context at a bigger timescale and links to a set of wider historical or social themes. Who Rosa Parks was and why what she did matters only has meaning if we know about the bigger context of the Equal Rights Movement; in biology, we go from organisms to organs to tissues to cells to cell structures and, finally, to biochemical processes. It's confusing to learn about osmosis in stomata guard cells unless we have a very clear understanding of the context of cells within a schema for plant structure and function. In poetry, in order to engage in a meaningful discussion of the specific meaning of, say, Ted Hughes's 'Suddenly, he awoke and was running – raw' (the opening line from 'Bayonet Charge'), it's going to be important to have some prior knowledge about the WWI context, and an understanding of a range of literary language techniques and structures as well as some background about Ted Hughes .

4. Provide models

Providing models is a central feature of giving good explanations. This has several meanings. Models can be:

- physical representations of completed tasks – exemplars that can be used as scaffolds, such as a model paragraph for opening a history essay.

- conceptual models – such as the one we need to form to understand the behaviour of particles in solids, liquids and gases.

- explicit narration of our thought processes when thinking through how to solve problems or undertake a creative activity.

There are lots of ways teachers can develop their practice by developing the way they provide models:

Link abstract ideas to concrete examples

This includes the use of physical manipulatives – blocks and shapes – when learning about numbers and fractions. An important example would be equivalent fractions – using diagrams or physical objects to build a model where ½ + ½ = ¼ + ¼ + 3/8 + 1/8. Another example is linking multiplication tables and division to a model:

$6 \times 4 = 24$. 4 rows of 6; 6 columns of 4. $24/6 = 4$ Children are well prepared for future learning if their schema for multiplication has a secure foundation of this kind.

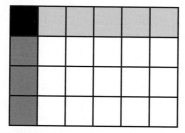

In science, using a molecular diagram and symbol equations to explain practical chemical reactions is essential, as with burning hydrocarbons:

Hydrocarbons + Oxygen → Carbon dioxide + Water

Methane: $CH_4 + 2O_2 \rightarrow CO_2 + 2H_2O$; the atoms are the same, but rearranged.

Atoms are the same, but rearranged

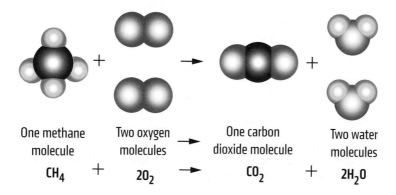

One methane molecule		Two oxygen molecules		One carbon dioxide molecule		Two water molecules
CH_4	+	$2O_2$	→	CO_2	+	$2H_2O$

In English, it's helpful to know concrete examples of technical grammar structures or features of writing. 'All of a sudden' is a fronted adverbial; 'She glided like a swan' is a simile; 'the wind swooshed and swirled around the houses' includes examples of onomatopoeia and alliteration. Moving to and fro between the abstract and the concrete is important in many aspects of language.

Link abstract knowledge to experiential 'tacit' knowledge

This builds directly on the section above. Concrete examples are often 'tacit'. As a science teacher, where the interplay of theory and practical work is well-rehearsed, I would extend Rosenshine's ideas into this important area – although it has implications in other subject domains.

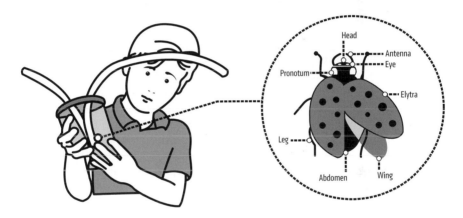

In the preamble to the ten principles, Rosenshine makes an important statement following a neat summary:

> The most effective teachers ensured that their students efficiently acquired, rehearsed, and connected background knowledge by providing a good deal of instructional support. They provided this support by teaching new material in manageable amounts, modeling, guiding student practice, helping students when they made errors, and providing for sufficient practice and review. Many of these teachers also went on to experiential, hands-on activities, but they always did the experiential activities *after,* not before, the basic material was learned.

I think this needs careful interpretation in different subject contexts. Rosenshine is firmly saying that some experiential activities are not successful in securing learning unless 'basic material' has been learned. Plenty of activities can seed confusion and misconceptions if students don't know enough about what they're doing. However, 'tacit' knowledge can also constitute the essential background or basic material that has to be learned. In my experience, many of the phenomena taught in science can be better understood once we've gained some tacit knowledge from hands-on experience in field studies, demonstrations or experiments. If we have studied insects by looking at them in a jar close up, then the technical work about labelling body parts and describing their form and function has a basis in our own reality. If we know what it feels like to control the speed of rotation of an electric motor, we are better placed to discuss the theoretical explanation. A well-sequenced curriculum will provide opportunities of this kind with hands-on activities in the most appropriate place to maximise learning.

Narrate the thought process

An important role for teachers is to support students in developing their capacity for metacognition and self-regulation[7] by modelling their own thought processes when engaging in a task. Effective teachers will be able to narrate the decisions and choices they make: where to begin with a maths problem; where to start with an essay; how to plan the timing of a 20-minute writing task; how to write in a style appropriate for a certain purpose and audience, making particular choices of words and phrases. By making the implicit explicit, teachers are supporting students to form their own mental models, gaining confidence with the decisions they make.

Organise the information

Modelling can help students to organise information into secure, well-structured schemata. As Shimamura suggests in the R of his MARGE[8] theory, we need to relate new knowledge to what we already know. He suggests that the three Cs – compare, contrast, categorise – can be helpful in doing this. Teachers can model the way complex sets of information can be sequenced, connected, and arranged into patterns to make it possible to learn and recall later.

7   Education Endowment Foundation www.bit.ly/2YZvdqE
8   Shimamura, A. (2018) MARGE *A Whole-Brain Learning Approach for Students and Teachers.* PDF available from www.bit.ly/2UEi1IB

An example of this might be to show how certain quotations in Shakespeare's *Macbeth* support the view of Macbeth as weak or guilt-ridden whereas others show him to be calculating and driven by ambition. Modelling the use of quotations provides a framework for students to engage in that process themselves.

Further examples would be any context where we might categorise advantages and disadvantages or arguments for and against and, more obviously, where categories relate to physical entities such as metals and non-metals or types of tectonic plate interactions. The more teachers illustrate the formation of relational models, the more likely it is that students will grasp the ideas and form sound schemata of their own.

Worked examples (aka worked-out examples)

As described briefly by Rosenshine, John Sweller and others have demonstrated the power of worked examples as an outcome of cognitive load theory. Effective teachers will tend to provide students with many worked examples so that the general patterns are clear, providing a strong basis from which to learn. The trick is then to gradually reduce the level of completion, leaving students to finish problems off and ultimately do them by themselves.

18% of £65	37% of £120	68% of £1050
$\dfrac{18}{100} \times 65$	$\dfrac{37}{100} \times 120$	$\dfrac{68}{100} \times 1050$
$= 0.18 \times 65$	$= 0.37 \times 120$	$= ? \times ?$
$= £11.70$	$= £44.40$	$= ?$

Rosenshine suggests that less effective teachers tend not to provide enough worked examples, thus adding to cognitive load as well as leaving students unsure of the procedures at hand and how to apply them.

Worked examples are powerful wherever calculations are involved but can also be used in any kind of structured writing or technical procedures, such as with grammar exercises in English or foreign languages, or balancing chemical equations. It's often the case that when I observe a teacher struggling to make headway with a class of students who seem stuck, I want to say 'show them another example'. So often this is the key to unlocking the next step in their understanding: seeing how it can be done.

8. Provide scaffolds for difficult tasks

Rosenshine tells us that it can be important for students to undergo a form of 'cognitive apprenticeship' whereby they learn cognitive strategies from a master teacher who models, coaches and supports them as they develop a level of independence. The key is that the scaffolds are temporary; they support the development of a cognitive process but are withdrawn so that students don't become reliant them. This is a form of guided practice as a precursor to independent practice. All of the ideas in the fourth principle ('Provide models') above can be used as temporary scaffolds that are later withdrawn.

A classic example of scaffolding is the use of stabilisers for learning to ride a bike. I had this experience with my own daughter. She found riding a bike difficult, so we put on stabilisers that allowed her to gain confidence with steering, pedalling, and the beginnings of balance. Then, we took the stabilisers off and I ran behind her holding the saddle. Eventually she called out, 'You can let go now, Dad!' The beautiful thing was, I already had! She was off, riding independently. The stabilisers and my saddle-holding had served their purpose as she moved through the learning process.

Writing frames

In the classroom, a common, useful tool is a writing frame to scaffold writing. This might be the use of an opening sentence for literary analysis:

- *Throughout the novel, the author...* – a structure that helps to discuss a long-running theme

- *At first glance, the character appears... However...* – a structure supporting comparison between surface and deep features of a character

- *Both poems... However, poem A... whereas poem B...* – a structure for comparing two poems

Writing frames can also be useful answering questions in science:

- *Initially, the concentration is...*

- *Then, as the level of X increases...*

- *This, in turn, causes...*

A very common feature of teaching in writing-heavy subjects is to provide paragraph structures as scaffolds:

- PEE: Point, Evidence, Explain

- SQuID: Statement, Quotation, Inference, Development

- PETAL: Point, Evidence, Technique, Analyse, Link

The idea is to teach students how to organise their ideas. For many students, this is critical to their success in developing their knowledge of forms of expression. However, if overused, there is a risk that these paragraphs read as very formulaic, so students need to be weaned off them as they reach higher levels where a greater degree of flair and individuality is expected. The whole point of scaffolding is that, eventually, it has to be taken down!

Exemplars

A useful form of scaffolds can be the examination of exemplars produced by previous students or by the teacher. Written success criteria can feel rather dense and difficult to interpret whereas the differences between exemplars of different standards can be much easier to understand. If students are asked for the positive features of an exemplar and ways it can be improved, and then asked to compare their own work to the exemplar, they can often make much better sense of the component elements that contribute to the idea of success. This can apply to writing or any creative process – an art piece or technology product.

Strategic thinking

In the question on the next page, many students who could answer the right-hand version would struggle with the left-hand version. This is simply because, in the apparent lack of any dimensions, they feel there is nothing they can do. The simple act of labelling the diagram provides a way into the problem. Once a radius is labelled, the area of the circle can be written as πr^2 and the square area can be seen to be $2r \times 2r$. However, students need to learn that they have the power to make the decision to undertake the labelling themselves; to introduce an algebraic variable and then use it. It's quite a big leap that needs modelling and scaffolding before students are able to do this independently with confidence.

What fraction is shaded?

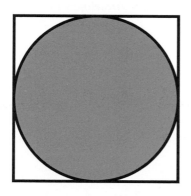 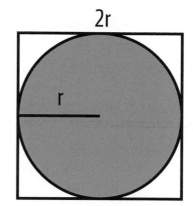

Most problem-solving subjects have a relatively small set of archetypal problems. Once students become familiar with them, their cognitive load is greatly reduced with subsequent encounters. In this sense, simply exposing students to multiple examples of the typical problem types scaffolds their capacity for problem-solving.

Anticipate errors and misconceptions.

An important aspect of modelling is to anticipate common errors and to explicitly challenge misconceptions. In maths and science, there are numerous well-known common misconceptions and errors; in writing, there are many common spelling and grammatical errors. A form of scaffolding is to tackle these things head-on, highlighting potential pitfalls and supporting students in checking their own work so that, ultimately, students have gained a sound knowledge of the pitfalls and are able to self-check and self-correct.

This could include basic numerical operations, such as keeping place value aligned in subtraction, multiplication and division; attending to the BIDMAS order of operations; checking for a positive increase when subtracting a negative number or when dividing by a number smaller than 1.

For writing, students can be provided with a checklist of common errors – full stops and capital letters, correct use of apostrophes – which students use initially and gradually stop relying on as they internalize the conventions.

In science, common misconceptions include the idea that the Earth's shadow causes the phases of the moon (it doesn't), that the mass of a tree comes from the soil (it comes from the air), or that 'cold' can flow into a house (it's heat that flows out, reducing the temperature inside; there is no such thing as 'cold' as an entity). In anticipating and teaching these ideas directly, students are able to form a more complete schema for the relevant topic.

STRAND 2: QUESTIONING

One of the strongest implications from Rosenshine's 'Principles of Instruction' is that effective questioning lies at the heart of great instructional teaching. Lined up with the work of Nuthall, Wiliam and others, it's clear that this needs to be a highly interactive, dynamic, responsive process.

Relevant instructional procedures include:

- Ask a large number of questions and check for understanding.
- Ask students to explain what they have learned.
- Check the response of all students.
- Provide systematic feedback and corrections.

3. Ask questions

Message sent

Message received?

Revisiting the notion that a class is essentially a room full of highly individual, easily distracted schema-forming brains grouped in front of us, it's vital that, as teachers, we are getting as much feedback from our students as we can. We cannot see the learning that is happening. But we can look for clues. We should be constantly wondering 'How's it going? How well have I explained this? Are they making sense of it?' and then soliciting information to allow us to answer those questions.

A strong message from Rosenshine is that more effective teachers ask more questions, involving more students, probing in more depth and taking more time to explain, clarify and check for understanding. In addition, they ask students to explain the process they have used to answer a question – to narrate their thinking. Significantly, 'less successful teachers ask fewer questions and almost no process questions'.

I have found a particular repertoire of questioning strategies useful for teachers to work on and the list below is what I usually work through in my training. In combination, these strategies unlock the full power of questioning, each seeking to achieve a particular objective. The idea is to work on one or two with deliberate practice until they form a set of organic, default modes for engaging in responsive teaching.

Cold calling (based on Lemov, Teach Like A Champion)

Objective: If we want all students to learn all the material then they should all be involved in engaging with the teacher-student dialogue with time to think, and not be allowed to hide, dominate or be overlooked.

Practice: No hands up! Teachers ask questions and then select students to respond based on their knowledge of the class, avoiding the pitfalls of hands-up or calling out. This is an inclusive process that conspicuously involves all students, front, back, in the corners, shy, confident – everyone. It's not a one-off strategy; ideally it needs to be the default mode for most questions – absolutely routine.

No opt-out (based on Lemov, Teach Like A Champion)

Objective: Students should feel safe in answering when unsure, but if they don't know or get things wrong, they should be given the opportunity to gain confidence by consolidating correct or secure answers. Also, students should not be allowed to form a defensive habit of saying 'I don't know' simply as a get-out.

Practice: If a student or several students get an answer completely or partially wrong or they say they don't know, move to other students or provide the correct answer. But then go back to all those students who made errors or couldn't answer, giving them a chance to now say the right answer. This gives them an opportunity for practice; but if done routinely, it also means that students soon learn there is no value in offering 'I don't know' as a defence in the hope of being left alone!

Say it again, better

Objective: It's normal for first responses to be half-formed as students think aloud and formulate ideas. A second opportunity to respond allows them to finesse their answers, adding depth, accuracy and sophistication. It's important not to inhibit students when they are unsure; it's also important not to allow them to assume mediocre answers are good enough.

Practice: When students offer short, half-formed or partially incorrect answers, say, 'Thanks, that's great. Now let's say it again better. Try again but make sure you add in X and link it to idea Y.' Allow them an immediate opportunity to give an improved response.

Think, pair, share

Objective: In pairs, you can give all students space to think, to air their initial thoughts, to confess their lack of knowledge and to prepare to give good answers, to rehearse. They are all involved and subsequent discussions then have lots of material to explore. It prevents 'blood out of a stone' silences inhibiting discussion and it prevents 'forest of hands', with students straining to get picked, or a culture of shouting out the answers from taking hold.

Practice: Give the class a specific time-cued task – for example, to decide on four main points in order of importance, in three minutes. Get them all talking in pairs and then, on time, bring them back together with a signal. Then engage in probing, cold-call questioning, asking them to report back what their four points were. You can also get them to explain things to each other or to take turns to quiz each other based on prompt sheets or a text.

Whole-class response

Objective: Sometimes it is useful or even essential to get a response from every single student at the same time. This provides quick feedback to you as the teacher about the success of the relevant teaching and learning exchanges, identifies individuals who need further input and can help direct subsequent questions or exercises as you respond to the feedback you gain.

Practice: My preference is for using whiteboards over any technology. They are cheap and quick and allow for responses to multiple-choice questions as well as practice sentences, calculations, diagrams – a full range. You set the question, give some response time and then, on cue – '3, 2, 1, show me!' – students all show their answers at once. A simple 'A, B, C, D = 1, 2, 3, 4' show of fingers also works very well for multiple-choice. It's vital to engage with the responses and then to adjust your teaching accordingly, consolidating, re-explaining or moving on as appropriate.

In situations where new vocabulary is being introduced, teachers can get good results from using tightly orchestrated choral repetition. Here, all students are involved, gaining confidence from the practice under cover of the class's collective voice.

Probing

Objective: In order to explore a student's schema in any depth, teachers need to ask them several questions. Merely asking a series of single questions in turn to several students provides shallow responses compared to when each student has provided multiple responses. Probing each student's schema with multiple responsive questions is a powerful mode of questioning and a form of guided practice.

Practice: Make it the default that, in any given exchange, you are asking each student three/four/five questions before moving on, probing for understanding, checking for misconceptions, adding extra challenge, providing scaffolding to engineer success. Rosenshine provides some good examples of this in 'Principles'. Here's my view of what a teacher might be saying in dialogue with students:

- That's interesting, what makes you say that?

- That's true, but why do you think that is?

- Is there a different way to say the same thing?

- Can you give an example of where that happens?

- Can you explain how you worked that out?

- So, what happens if we make it bigger or smaller?

- Why? Are you sure? Is there another explanation?

- Which of those things makes the biggest impact?

- What is the theme that links all those ideas together?

- What is the evidence that supports that suggestion?

- Does anyone agree with that? Why?

- Does anyone disagree? What would you say instead? Why is that different?

- How does that answer compare to that answer?

- But what's the reason for that? And how is that connected to the first part?

- How did you know that? What made you think of that? Where did that idea come from?

- Is that always true or just in this example?

- What would be the opposite of that?

- Is it true for everyone or just some people?

- Is that a direct cause of the effect or is it just a coincidence, a correlation?

6. Check for student understanding

In the 1982 paper, standing out in the whole list of teaching functions, Rosenshine underlines 'checks for understanding', adopting the abbreviation CFU. This appears to be at the centre of the whole process – something I'd wholeheartedly support from my experience observing and teaching hundreds of lessons. For me, it's the core concept in the Principles. Based on my recent work as a teacher trainer, I'd suggest that CFU is probably the single biggest common area for improvement in the teaching that I see – so I'm happy to see Rosenshine literally underlining it as being important. (Unsurprisingly, it's also a prominent theme in Doug Lemov's *Teach Like a Champion*.)

Here is a superb excerpt from *Teaching Functions* where Rosenshine explains how *not* to do CFU:

> The wrong way to check for understanding is to ask only a few questions, call on volunteers to hear their (usually correct) answers, and then

assume that all of the class either understands or has now learned from hearing the volunteers' responses. Another error is to ask, 'Are there any questions?' and, if there aren't any, assume that everybody understands. Another error (particularly with older children) is to assume that it is not necessary to check for understanding, and that simply repeating the points will be sufficient.

I love this. It's all too common. A scenario I often use to highlight this problem is to ask people to imagine the process of teaching something with high-stakes outcomes like abseiling. If your goal is for your team of novice abseilers to abseil independently – safely reaching the ground – you would go a lot further than simply demonstrating the technique and asking 'Are there any questions?' or assuming one student's correct modelling of the procedure indicated the likely success of the others. You would definitely check that everyone could do it and give them all plenty of practice.

And yet, in lessons, teachers use these rhetorical, self-report questions and crude assumptions of understanding all the time – with adding fractions or conjugating verbs! It's high risk, in learning terms.

If we are going to be sure all students have formed secure understanding, teachers should not assume that knowledge aired and shared in the public space of the classroom has been absorbed and learned by any individual. It's necessary to

Why does the sun rise in the east?

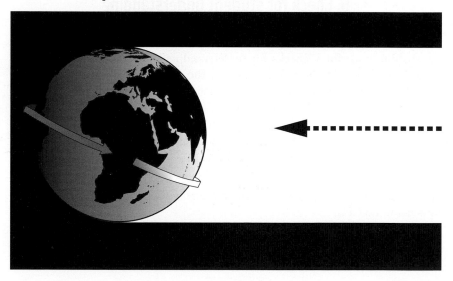

check for understanding from students to determine whether they understood what you meant. Do they now have the level of understanding you are aiming at?

An example might be similar to the question I often use in my training: why does the sun rise in the east? People often think they know this – until they start to explain it to someone else!

The process we undertake in answering a question like this is to generate a new version of what we've previously learned. We then evaluate that version to determine if it is complete and correct. A silent self-checking process is powerful in itself but we might also get the class to explain to each other in pairs. This helps to engage everyone. The teacher can then sample the class to check the understanding of individuals. Importantly, they should be asking the student to run through their whole explanation to determine the accuracy of their schema, not just a small part of it.

After any exposition or question exchange with a particular student, the process suggested by 'Principles of Instruction' is that teachers should ask a number of other students to relay back what they have understood. Always, instead of 'Have you understood?', you should ask 'Can you tell me what you have understood?' It's a radically different question.

Have you understood? Vs What have you understood?

Even if they are answering a question that someone else has already answered, it's valuable for other students to be given a chance to offer their version, showing what they have understood and, in so doing, giving the teacher feedback about how successful the teaching has been. It's especially powerful to ask multiple students, often yielding various different responses which throw up subtle points for further teaching. This can be combined with all-student response questioning with mini whiteboards or other short writing tasks where everyone generates a response to show their understanding as the teacher circulates the class.

There are two key benefits from checking for understanding:

1. The teacher gains feedback about which part of the material might need to be revisited, re-taught or given more practice time.

2. In rehearsing their understanding, students are likely to be elaborating on the knowledge in the relevant schemata which will strengthen connections between different ideas and improve long-term retention. The checking helps them remember more the next time they check.

Rosenshine suggests that the importance of checking for understanding reinforces the need to present material in small steps. If we allow students to try to construct a mental summary of too much material at once, they can introduce errors that then become stored in their schemata as learned misconceptions. This is especially true where students' prior background knowledge is weak for a given concept. If we check for understanding with smaller amounts of material, we're likely to be supporting students in forming stronger, more reliable schemata.

Checking for understanding can work at a general overview level to support teacher instruction but it can become quite forensic when we are focusing on maximising individual success. For example, a teacher might construct a definitive answer following a class discussion or predetermine what a good answer should contain. They can then use this as a focus for their CFU process as students write individual answers or explain verbally.

Why does the sun rise in the east?	Success?
Before sunrise, **the Sun is at a distance**, not visible to the part of the Earth experiencing night.	
Earth rotates anticlockwise (looking from North Pole).	
As night moves to day, the Sun appears on **east horizon** – to our left if we stand facing south.	
The **impression of 'rising' is an illusion**; it is the Earth rotating relative to the Earth-Sun line.	

In general, I would advocate placing 'Checking for understanding' right at the centre of teachers' thinking during their lessons. It forces us to consider the detail of what we want all students to know and how, exactly, to organise the lesson to maximise the number and the depth of student responses we can engage with.

STRAND 3: REVIEWING MATERIAL

A major issue in learning is the inevitable, predictable and natural process of forgetting. Unless we review what we've learned, our memory of that information diminishes: we remember fewer details, fewer connections and find it harder to retrieve what we previously learned. Retrieval practice supports building our long-term memory and our level of fluency in recall.

Relevant instructional procedures from Rosenshine include:

- Begin a lesson with a short review of previous learning.
- Re-teach material when necessary.

1. Daily review

One of the purposes of daily review is to support the development of fluency as explored below with weekly and monthly review. The significance of daily review is that it allows students to re-activate recently acquired knowledge, reducing cognitive load at the beginning of a lesson that's designed to build on this knowledge. Students don't necessarily recall recent learning readily and it pays to anticipate this rather than be frustrated by it. It's also important for prior learning to be active in our working memory if we're going to add more layers of complexity to it; the connections we want to engineer won't happen otherwise.

A very common example might be the use of new terminology or vocabulary. It might be that yesterday we learned the new word 'sesquipedalian' – meaning 'tending to use long words; long-winded'. Today, we want to use knowledge of that word to explore a text. We could start the lesson with a multiple-choice question which everyone is required to answer independently, justifying their choice of correct response and all the incorrect responses. It's not just a case of saying 'Does everyone remember what we learned yesterday?' The question makes the students explore their understanding.

For example:

> Which sentence uses the word 'sesquipedalian' most appropriately?
>
> A. Sesquipedalian people are in their seventies.
>
> B. The man felt sesquipedalian after his operation.
>
> C. John was a rather sesquipedalian speaker; his audiences would sometimes lose focus.
>
> D. The speech was full of sesquipedalian facts that didn't support her main argument.

Another example might be the use of quotation from a literacy text:

> Based on yesterday's lesson, complete the quotation and then, in a pair, discuss the significance of this quotation from Act 3: Scene 2 in *Macbeth*.
>
> 'O, full of _____ is _____, _____.'
> (O, full of scorpions is my mind, dear wife.)

We might also ask students for some straightforward factual recall:

- We learned five key advantages of wind power over coal-fired power. What were they?

- We practised some angle facts questions yesterday. Try the three questions on the slide to refresh your memory. The first one is partially completed to get you started.

As cognitive scientist Efrat Furst explains in her work[9] on understanding 'understanding' and reconsolidation of memory, there is a natural time delay factor that teachers should take account of in their teaching. It's entirely natural for students to experience some short-term confusion and lack of fluency as they encounter new material because we don't re-wire our brains instantaneously. A daily review routine can serve the purpose of checking in to see that, with some time having passed, students have secured the knowledge required in their memory in good enough shape to go build on it further.

---

9   Efrat Furst on consolidation: www.bit.ly/2U9xMDf

10. Weekly and monthly review

One main purpose of weekly and monthly review is to ensure that previously learned material is not forgotten – to attenuate the natural rate of forgetting. It is also to ensure that, through frequent revisiting of a range of material, students are able to form ever more well-connected networks of ideas – more extensive schemata. This form of practice helps students to learn more information and makes it easier to be successful with problem-solving as less space in short-term memory is needed.

More effective teachers routinely engage students in a variety of forms of retrieval practice, recalling and applying previously learned material.

In this example, suppose that we want all students to know some key events in the history of the civil rights movement, including the dates. A task might be to get them to study the timeline notes on the left and then, the following week, to get them to complete the blank dates for the shuffled set of events on the right. This is something they can practise at home and can check for themselves. Where possible, if students can check their own answers, so much the better. A week later, we might give them a table of dates and ask students to fill in the events, to mix up the way in which the material is being tested.

1955	Montgomery bus boycott	Civil Rights Act	?
1960	Freedom Summer	Freedom Summer	?
1963	March on Washington	March on Washington	?
1964	Civil Rights Act	MLK Assassinated	?
1965	Rise of Black Power	Montgomery bus boycott	?
1968	MLK Assassinated	Rise of Black Power	?

Of course, knowing the dates is only the baseline for more advanced pieces of work. The idea is that where students have more fluent recall of these basic facts, they have more space in working memory to attend to applying the knowledge to explain deeper questions.

Another form of retrieval practice is utilising the memory-building power of narrative structures. It's not all about simple recall tests! One example could be to review understanding and recall of the water cycle. Students are asked to tell the story of a water molecule, starting in the sea, using the correct terminology for changes of state and using the concept of energy.

Tell the story...

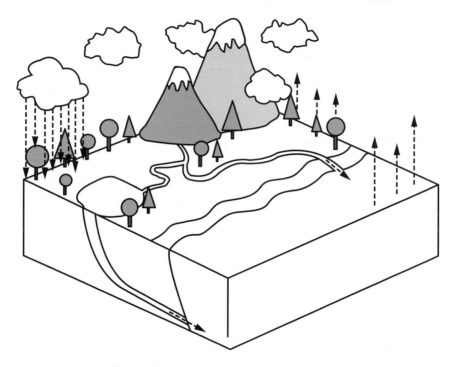

Students then, individually or in pairs, engage in elaborative-interrogative questioning. 'How does this happen?' 'Why did that happen?' This type of questioning has been shown to have a strong effect on future retention[10] as it forces us to form more coherent schemata.

Finally, it's important to remember that we are all prey to the illusion of familiarity. As Shimamura explains in the G and E of MARGE[11] – generate and evaluate – we can easily think we've learned something if the information is continually presented to us. We see ideas laid out that we recognise so we tell ourselves that we've learned them. However, in order to evaluate our recall and understanding, we must generate versions of that information from memory without looking at the source. This tells us, as the learner, what we know and don't know – even before our teacher gets to find out.

---

10   Sumeracki, M. and Weinstein, Y (2018)
11   Shimamura, A (2018)

An example I've explored for myself is the process of learning key facts and narratives about the famous story of King Henry VIII's six wives. Having read about them several times, I nonetheless found myself forgetting key details. So, in order to strengthen my recall, I re-studied the material focusing on more specific information – names, marriage dates, their fate – and then generated this timeline from memory. I evaluated the information I generated from memory by checking with the source, adding and correcting details and repeating the process several days later. It worked!

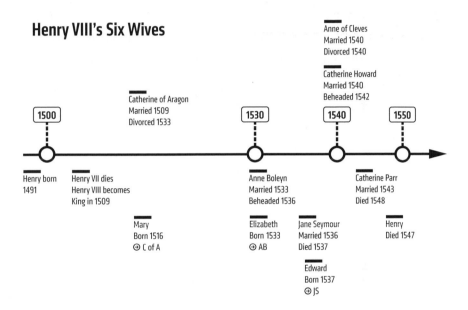

I found that it helped me to recall the information as I added more layers of narrative around each of the women. Once Anne Boleyn or Catherine Howard have distinctive characters and life stories, they cease to be bland names on a page; the schemata I have for them are more complete and I have more connections to other schemata, the basis for fluency.

More generally, the idea that learning is a *generative process* is important. Daily, weekly and monthly review activities give students opportunities to generate versions of what they know and understand, helping to strengthen future retrieval of the knowledge involved, build fluency, and identify where they might have residual gaps or areas of uncertainty.

In summary, to make daily, weekly and monthly review part of an effective and sustainable routine, I suggest that the following principles should apply:

- **Involve everyone:** Good techniques involve all students checking their knowledge, not just a few and not just one at a time as you might do when questioning.

- **Make checking accurate and easy:** it should be possible for all students to find out what they got right and wrong, what they know well and where they have gaps. Good techniques involve students testing their knowledge and then checking their work for accuracy and completeness. This is not the same as giving students extended mark schemes to mark longer assessments which are beyond a simple retrieval practice activity.

- **Specify the knowledge:** Where appropriate, it's better if students know the set of knowledge any retrieval will be based on, so they can study, prepare and self-check. It must be possible for students to check their own answers, which has implications for the way the knowledge requirements are laid out.

- **Keep it generative:** students need to explore their memory to check what they know and understand. This means removing cue-cards, prompts, scaffolds and cheat-sheets; it means closing the books and making students think for themselves.

- **Vary the diet:** mix up the use of teacher-led, self-quizzing, written and verbal quizzing, self-explanation, 'telling the story', multiple-choice and open-response tests, rehearsing explanations, summarising, creating knowledge maps, demonstration and performance of learned techniques, routines and procedures. This will allow students to explore their schemata in different ways, strengthening future recall.

- **Make it time efficient:** A good technique can be used repeatedly in an efficient manner without dominating whole lessons.

- **Make it workload efficient:** The best methods do not involve the teacher checking the students' answers, creating unsustainable workload. A teacher might choose to check the occasional test but for routine practice, students should do it themselves.

STRAND 4: STAGES OF PRACTICE

One of the reasons I am such a big fan of Rosenshine's 'Principles of Instruction' is that it brings the idea of practice to the fore. As a profession, we have been through a period where ideas such as rote learning, repetition or drill have been disparaged and scoffed at as old-fashioned – even characterised as being against the spirit of great learning. But once you de-demonise these ideas, reconstituting them simply as 'practice', they seem entirely sensible as part of a sound learning process. Nobody ever excels at anything without lots of practice and that starts with the way we conduct our lessons.

Relevant instructional procedures include:

- Provide a high level of practice for all students.
- Guide students as they begin to practice.
- Prepare students for independent practice.
- Monitor students when they begin independent practice.

The distinction between guided practice and independent practice is a hallmark of Rosenshine's thinking.

5. Guide student practice

Rosenshine suggests that, in the observational research, the most effective teachers gave more time for guided practice – which is directly linked to them spending more time asking questions, more time checking for understanding and using more worked examples. The idea is that if students are going to be successful in becoming confident and independent within a certain knowledge area, the teacher needs to make sure they are forming a strong schema early on.

Importantly, we actually need a broad view of what might constitute 'practice'. In this section of 'Principles', Rosenshine says: 'An important finding from information-processing research is that students need to spend additional time rephrasing, elaborating, and summarizing new material in order to store this material in their long-term memory.' This gives us a steer as to the kinds of cognitive processes students might engage in when practising. There are many ways to revisit material so that the schema-forming process is successful.

All students need to practise – but that practice must be guided so that the chance of forming misconceptions is minimised. Not only that: the guidance is key to generating the high success rate that in turn fuels motivation and engagement during more independent work. The less confident learners are, and the less prior knowledge they have, then the more important guided practice is. As students gain in knowledge and confidence, the guided practice phase can become shorter or can cover large amounts of material at once.

In essence, guided practice is typically where learning activities involve thorough explanations, high-frequency, short-answer questions or simple tasks where the teacher and students are engaged interactively, with plenty of modelling, corrective or affirming feedback and aspects of re-teaching where gaps remain. If students are involved in what Rosenshine calls 'seatwork' then the teacher would be circulating, looking closely at student responses to check for early errors or successes. With insufficient early practice or guidance, students often flounder with subsequent independent tasks.

Guided practice can be applied to learning in so many ways, building fluency and ultimately developing a level of automaticity with recall. To a great extent, asking questions and checking for understanding, as described earlier, are forms of guided practice. The ideas explored for modelling and scaffolding are all part of guiding practice. It's here that the Principles of Instruction strongly overlap and reinforce each other.

One of the issues teachers sometimes have is in generating a high level of repetition that involves all students. As well as the more obvious method of setting exercises with multiple questions of the same type, I have seen teachers make excellent use of choral repetition and quick-fire questioning to achieve high-frequency repetition including the following:

Fronted adverbials for dramatic impact: students practise these sentences, repeatedly stating the stem with each variation that they made up:

- Quick as a flash…
  - → …he disappeared behind the fence.
  - → …he climbed the tower.
  - → …she conjured up a potion.

- All of a sudden…

    → …she fell down a hole.

    → …giant hailstones began to fall.

    → …he changed his mood.

Students are less likely to use phrases independently if they have not had a chance to practise them first.

Number bonds to 100: The teacher calls out a number 0–100 and the students chant back the bond to hundred – (easily then extended to 1000 or any other number):

56 … 44!

87 … 13!

23 … 77!

This was an activity that students did frequently so the objective was to increase fluency through the speed of response. The more often they do it, the better they get.

Choral repetition: In a French lesson, students learn a new phrase and how to say it with a good accent by using it themselves repeatedly. The guided practice phase involves whole-class choral repetition with the teacher first modelling the French but then switching to give only the English.

Où que j'aille : Où que j'aille (Wherever I go)

Quoi que je fasse : Quoi que je fasse (Whatever I do)

Où que j'aille, quoi que je fasse : Où que j'aille, quoi que je fasse

Wherever I go : Où que j'aille

Whatever I do : Quoi que je fasse

Wherever I go, whatever I do : Où que j'aille, quoi que je fasse

Wherever I go, whatever I do, the sun always shines : Où que j'aille, quoi que je fasse, le soleil brille toujours

Wherever I go, whatever I do, I always find litter : Où que j'aille, quoi que je fasse, je trouve toujours des déchets

The choral work is often punctuated with selecting individuals to respond, picking up on details of syntax and pronunciation. The confidence-building that comes from these activities is significant.

A common feature of practice is repetition. Sometimes practice activities are unsuccessful because students are practising too many things at one time and, therefore, they are not practising any one thing often enough. This can be true in languages lessons where too many new words and grammar features are being practised; it can be true of extended writing tasks where students are wrestling with the content, structure, language, grammar – and flounder under the weight of it all. The trick is to break down tasks as suggested by principle 2, so that repeated practice of smaller steps can be achieved before they are assimilated into more complex tasks.

7. Obtain a high success rate

The research Rosenshine refers to includes studies that show that more effective teachers set questions and tasks with sufficient practice to engineer a high success rate – with an optimal level around 80% success. He even suggests that going down to 70% is too low. If students are getting too much wrong, then they are effectively practising making errors! This can then form part of what is learned and be hard to overcome.

The idea is that at 80% most of what students are doing is reinforcing error-free, secure learning, improving fluency and confidence. This then provides a stronger platform for subsequent learning. However, we are not talking about 90–95% in the early stages. It's important that students are challenged; that they have learning goals that are ahead of them. It's a well-established aspect of the growth mindset research[12] that, in order to succeed, students need to approach challenge with a positive attitude, understanding how to learn from mistakes and not be afraid of making them. This is how we reach high levels of achievement: we stretch beyond our current capabilities, working hard at a strategy until it yields success or changing strategy to find another path to success. We then practise that successful strategy to increase fluency and push on again. It's as much about strategy as about effort.

The implication for teachers is that we need to continually evaluate the success rate of our students:

> If their success rate is too low, we may need to go back: to re-teach, re-explain, re-model; to return to more secure ground and build back up again, perhaps trying different approaches. We then need to give students more guided practice at a strategy that allows them to reach the nominal 80% threshold. Nothing new, just more practice.

---

12   e.g. www.bit.ly/2Di6813

If their success is much higher than 80%, it suggests they are ready for more challenge. We need to add levels of depth in the knowledge requirements in the task, to set more difficult problems, to require deeper explanations, to remove some of the scaffolds and supports.

In my view, it's unrealistic to achieve this neatly for all students in a mixed-attainment class, minute by minute. The 80% goal is more appropriate as an overarching benchmark over the course of a series of lessons – supporting more here, challenging more there, nudging, stretching, pushing, giving clues, adding support, taking support away. It's a combination of the minutiae of classroom interactions with planning of tasks and resources that allow for success at different rates or degrees of depth depending on where students are in their learning. Also, as we reach the conclusion of a topic, you might well expect students to be getting closer to 100% right on a knowledge test. That would be the explicit goal.

9. Independent practice

In many ways, this is the ultimate goal for teaching: to construct learning so that students are able to do challenging things by themselves without help. 'The more successful teachers provided for extensive and successful practice, both in the classroom and after class.' Less effective teachers may not only cut guided practice short, they also do not provide enough opportunity for independent practice. Judging the transition from students being guided enough to becoming independent is a subtle skill, a central element of teacher expertise that develops with knowing the material, knowing how to break it down into practicable elements and, crucially, knowing the students.

Rosenshine suggests that it is important for the material that students practise to be the same during independent practice as during guided practice in order for the appropriate level of success to be secured. During independent practice, success rates need to be as high as possible, especially if the teacher is not present to provide corrective feedback.

The basic flow of many learning experiences is this:

- Teacher explains.
- Teacher models.
- Teacher checks for understanding.

- Student engages in guided practice with scaffolding as needed.

- Scaffolding and support are gradually withdrawn.

- Student engages in independent practice.

- Student becomes fluent.

A simpler version that I like is: I do it; we do it; you do it: I. We. You. However we express it, it is vital that students are given ample opportunities to perform tasks by themselves. This applies to using new vocabulary in speech or writing, performing mathematical operations, explaining any kind of natural phenomenon, telling a story, making an argument, playing a piece of music, performing a piece of theatre or dance.

I've seen a great example of this not working well. A Year 1 teacher was trying to teach her students to broaden their vocabulary, working around a well-known witches story. On the board, there were various words and suggestions captured during class discussion. The teacher was aiming at something like: 'The wicked witch had gnarled fingers and terrible twisted toes.'

We came into the class as visitors and the teacher selected a student to showcase their work.

Teacher: Janine, tell the visitors what we know about the witch.

Janine: The witch was really bad.

The teacher was crestfallen. But the problem was obvious. Janine had not had nearly enough independent practice using the target words to gain a level of confidence and fluency. Under pressure to perform, she reverted to her confidence base – her more basic vocabulary. I see this kind of thing all the time.

I've seen many excellent examples including the use of well-structured collaborative learning – or 'cooperative learning' as Rosenshine calls it. One example was students practising how to explain how a transformer works after a guided practice phase involving teacher questioning. This has about six major steps running from an input voltage to an output voltage via an iron core and various coils and magnetic fields. One student in each pair had their knowledge organiser that detailed each step alongside a labelled diagram; the partner student had a blank diagram. Without notes, the task was to rehearse the full explanation in detail, giving the student an opportunity to practise generating, elaborating and communicating the details of their mental model of the process; the partner served as a verifier. They then swapped and later applied the same process to other electromagnetic devices.

Other simple examples include: French lessons where students are tasked to engage in dialogues based on their recent learning without using their notes; maths lessons where students simply attempt extensive problem sets building on their recent learning; English lessons where students write paragraphs or essays without structured supports, consolidating the knowledge content and techniques they have just acquired.

An essential feature of independent practice is that students draw on their own resources. This is where they have to rely on recall from memory, building fluency through repeatedly engaging in processes that reinforce connections and retrieval pathways, generating their own feedback and setting their own goals for improvement. The teacher's role is to provide students with the tools they need to do this, including teaching them explicit strategies for checking their own work against a set of standards in a form they can understand, using exemplars, mark schemes and so on.

CONCLUSION

As a teacher and teacher-trainer, I have found that Barak Rosenshine's Principles of Instruction provide a superb structure for supporting the process of professional development. As is evident reading the 'Principles' paper, all the principles overlap: several key ideas around practice and the ways cognitive processes link to classroom activities are repeated in each section. However, it is useful to consider each strand one by one:

- Sequencing concepts and modelling
- Questioning
- Reviewing material
- Stages of practice

In each case, the question we should ask is not 'Do we do this?' Most teachers will say that they do. We all ask questions; we all get students to practise; we all try to sequence concepts in small steps. The question we should ask is '*How well* do we do this?' For me, this is where the power of 'Principles of Instruction' lies, because we can all get better at delivering on each strand:

- We can all find better ways to sequence concepts with more effective models and forms of scaffolding.
- We can all increase the intensity of questioning and the depth of checking for understanding, increasing the ratio of students involved.
- We can all improve our efficiency and success with reviewing material, securing better levels of retention and more sophisticated responses.
- We can all develop ever-better ways of engineering high success rates as we move skilfully from guided to independent practice.

Importantly, it is unrealistic and unhelpful to work on each of these improvement agendas simultaneously. Teachers and their leaders should use 'Principles of Instruction' as a source of guidance and a self-reflection tool but it will be important to get better at one thing at time.

It's also important to recognise that most subjects require a diet of activities and lesson types that vary over time and it would not be reasonable or sensible to expect to see each of these principles being modelled during any given one-off lesson observation. Please, please, please do not corrupt the spirit and intent of 'Principles of Instruction' by turning it into a lesson-by-lesson checklist. Use it to lift people up, not to tie them down!

Finally, it's essential that we develop subject-specific models around it. We already suffer enough genericism in education and it would be a mistake to seek to impose a 'Principles of Instruction' formula of some kind into areas that it does not belong. For each subject domain, teachers should consider how the principles or the four strands apply. There is always knowledge; there is always practice; there is always a role for checking for understanding – but the way these things take form varies significantly from physics to Spanish to history to art to drama to maths and to science. Let's celebrate that variety and not seek to confine it.

Thank you to Barak Rosenshine for the gift you've given us in 'Principles of Instruction'. I have already met many hundreds of teachers who have found it immensely supportive in making their day-to-day work in the classroom more rewarding and more productive as they seek to lead their students to excellence, and I know for sure there will thousands more to follow in future.

REFERENCES

Deans for Impact (2016). *Practice with Purpose: The Emerging Science of Teacher Expertise*. Austin, TX: Deans for Impact.

Furst, E. (2019) *Understanding 'Understanding'*. Blog post www.bit.ly/2U9xMDf

Hattie, J. (2009) *Visible Learning: A synthesis of over 800 meta-analyses relating to achievement*. Routledge.

Lemov, D. (2015) *Teach Like A Champion 2.0 : 62 Techniques That Put Students On The Path To College*. Jossey-Bass. San Francisco, USA.

Nuthall, G (2007) *The Hidden Lives of Learners*, NZCER Press, Wellington NZ

Quigley, A. Muijs, D and Stringer, E. (2018) *Metacognition and Self-Regulated Learning Guidance Report*. Education Endowment Foundation

Rosenshine, B. (1982) *Teaching Functions in Instructional Programmes*. National Institute of Education. Washington, DC

Rosenshine, B. (1986) *Teaching Functions*. In M.C. WITTROCK (dir.), Handbook of Research on Teaching, 3e éd., New York, Macmillan, p. 376-391, 1986.

Rosenshine, B. (2010) 'Principles of Instruction', The International Academy of Education (IAE) *Educational Practices* Series 21 .

Rosenshine, B. (2012) 'Principles of Instruction: Research-based Strategies that all Teachers Should Know', *American Educator* Spring. 2012

Shimamura, A. (2018) *MARGE A Whole-Brain Learning Approach for Students and Teachers*. PDF available from www.bit.ly/2UEi1IB

Sumeracki, M. and Weinstein, Y. with Caviglioli, O. (2018) *Understanding how we learn – a Visual Guide* Routledge.

Sweller, J., Ayres. P., Kalyuga, S. (2011) *Cognitive Load Theory* Springer

Wiliam, D. (2011) *Embedded Formative Assessment* Solution Tree Press

Willingham, D. (2009) *Why don't students like school?* Jossey-Bass

Yeager, D. et al (2013) '*Addressing achievement gaps with psychological interventions' Kappan* February 2013.

ACKNOWLEDGEMENTS

I owe the existence of this book to several people. First of all, Barak Rosenshine himself for obvious reasons! I hope I've done his work justice. Then Oliver Caviglioli who drew my attention to Rosenshine's principles through his superb graphics. I'm thrilled that he found time to produce illustrations for this book alongside his many other projects. The idea for the book itself came from Mark Combes at Learning Sciences International in the US. He saw me give my Rosenshine talk at the 2018 ResearchEd event in Philadelphia organised by Eric Kalenze and felt that a short 'explainer' for teachers in the US might be useful. So this book would not exist without Mark and Eric or Tom Bennett, who has supported my involvement in ResearchEd events many times.

The UK edition has been enthusiastically embraced by Alex Sharratt at John Catt with the superb editorial oversight of Jonathan Woolgar. The US edition has been driven along by Dana Lake. I'm grateful for their support through the whole process.

I'd like to acknowledge some of the people who have helped me get to grips with the concepts in the book, directly or indirectly: Arthur Shimamura, Efrat Furst, Daniel Willingham, Paul Kirschner, David Didau and Nick Rose have helped me to develop a deeper understanding of learning processes. Finally, the staff at Oldham College and Brune Park School and my wife and Deputy Headteacher Deborah O'Connor have all helped me formulate ideas about putting theory into practice.

ROSENSHINE'S 'PRINCIPLES OF INSTRUCTION'

Barak Rosenshine (1930–2017) began his career as a high school history teacher before studying for a PhD at Stanford University and then becoming a professor in the Department of Educational Psychology at the University of Illinois. Here, his research focused on learning instruction, teacher performance, and student achievement.

In 2010, the International Academy of Education (IAE) published Rosenshine's summary of his research in the form of ten 'Principles of Instruction' as part of their Educational Practices series. That paper was popularised by *American Educator* magazine in 2012 and is the subject of this book. In the following pages, the paper is reprinted in full. Readers may find it useful to refer to the original paper alongside the discussion as presented in my four strands in the first part of this book.

Table of contents

Introduction

This pamphlet presents ten research-based principles of instruction, and suggestions for classroom practice. These principles come from three sources: (a) research on how our brain acquires and uses new information; (b) research on the classroom practices of those teachers whose students show the highest gains; and (c) findings from studies that taught learning strategies to students.

The first source of these suggestions is research in cognitive science. This research focuses on how our brains acquire and use information. This cognitive research also provides suggestions on how we might overcome the limitations of our working memory when learning new material. These suggestions appear in these ten principles.

A second source of the instructional ideas in this pamphlet comes from observing the classroom practices of master teachers. Master teachers are those teachers whose classrooms made the highest gains on achievement tests. These teachers were observed as they taught, and the investigators coded how they presented new material, how and whether they checked for student understanding, the types of support they provided to their students and a number of other instructional activities. The activities that were used by the most-successful teachers are incorporated into these ten principles.

A third source of suggestions for classroom practice came from the research of cognitive scientists who developed and tested cognitive supports and scaffolds that helped students learn complex tasks. Instructional procedures, such as thinking aloud, providing students with scaffolds and providing students with models, came from this research and these procedures are also described in these ten principles.

Each of these three sources has suggestions for classroom practice that are included in this pamphlet. An interesting finding is that there is no conflict at all between the instructional suggestions that come from each of these three sources. In other words, these three sources supplement and complement each other. And the fact that the instructional ideas from three different sources supplement and complement each other gives us faith in the validity of these findings.

The following is a list of some of the instructional procedures that have come from these three sources. These ideas will be described and discussed in this pamphlet:

- Begin a lesson with a short review of previous learning.

- Present new material in small steps with student practice after each step.

- Limit the amount of material students receive at one time.

- Give clear and detailed instructions and explanations.

- Ask a large number of questions and check for understanding.

- Provide a high level of active practice for all students.

- Guide students as they begin to practice.

- Think aloud and model steps.

- Provide models of worked-out problems.

- Ask students to explain what they had learned.

- Check the responses of all students.

- Provide systematic feedback and corrections.

- Use more time to provide explanations.

- Provide many examples.

- Re-teach material when necessary.

- Prepare students for independent practice.

- Monitor students when they begin independent practice.

1. Daily review

Daily review can strengthen previous learning and can lead to fluent recall.

Research findings

Daily review is an important component of instruction. Review can help us to strengthen the connections of the material we have learned. The review of previous learning can help us to recall words, concepts and procedures effortlessly and automatically when we need this material to solve problems or to understand new material. The development of expertise requires thousands of hours of practice and daily review is one component of this practice.

Daily review was part of a successful experiment in elementary school mathematics. Teachers in the experiment were taught to spend eight minutes every day on review. Teachers used this time to check the homework, go over problems where there were errors, and practise the concepts and skills that needed to be practised until they became automatic. As a result, students in these classrooms had higher achievement scores than did students in other classrooms.

Daily practice of vocabulary can lead to seeing the words as a unit, to seeing the whole word automatically rather than as individual letters. When students see words as a unit, they have more space available in their working memory, and this space can now be used for comprehension. Mathematical problem-solving is also improved when the basic skills (addition, multiplication, etc.) are overlearned and become automatic, thus freeing memory capacity.

In the classroom

The most effective teachers in the studies of classroom instruction understood the importance of practice and they would begin their lessons with a five- to eight-minute review of previously covered material. Some teachers would review vocabulary, or formulae, or events or previously learned concepts. These teachers provided additional practice on facts and skills that were needed for recall to become automatic.

Teacher activities might also include reviewing the concepts and skills that were necessary to do the homework, having students correct each others' papers, asking about points over which the students had difficulty or made errors, and reviewing or providing additional practice on facts and skills that need overlearning. These reviews ensured that the students had a firm grasp of the skills and concepts that would be needed for the day's lesson.

Effective teachers also reviewed the knowledge and concepts that are relevant for that day's lesson. It is important for a teacher to help students recall the concepts and vocabulary that will be relevant for the day's lesson, because our working memory is small. If we do not review previous learning, then we will have to make a special effort to recall old material while we are learning new material, and this process will make it difficult for students to learn the new material.

Daily review is particularly important for teaching material that will be used in subsequent learning. Examples include reading sight words (i.e. any word that is known by a reader automatically), grammar, math facts, math computation, math factoring and chemical equations.

When planning for review, teachers might want to consider which words, math facts, procedures and concepts need to become automatic, and which words, vocabulary or ideas need to be reviewed before the lesson begins.

In addition, teachers might consider doing the following during their daily review:

- Correction of homework;
- Review of the concepts and skills that were practised as part of the homework;
- Asking students about points where they had difficulties or made errors;
- Review of material where errors were made;
- Review of material that needs overlearning (i.e. newly acquired skills should be practised well beyond the point of initial mastery, leading to automaticity).

Suggested readings: Miller, 1956; LaBerge & Samuels, 1974.

2. Present new material using small steps

Only present small amounts of new material at any time,
and then assist students as they practise this material.

Research findings

Our working memory, the place where we process information, is small. It can only handle a few bits of information at once—too much information swamps our working memory. Presenting too much material at once may confuse students because their short-term memory will be unable to process it.

Therefore, the more effective teachers do not overwhelm their students by presenting too much new material at once. Rather, these teachers only present small amounts of new material at any time, and then assist the students as they practise this material. Only after the students have mastered the first step do teachers proceed to the next step.

The procedure of first teaching in small steps and then guiding student practice represents an appropriate way of dealing with the limitation of our working memory.

In the classroom

The more-successful teachers did not overwhelm their students by presenting too much new material at once. Rather, they only presented small amounts of new material at one time, and they taught in such a way that each point was mastered before the next point was introduced. They checked their students' understanding on each point and re-taught material when necessary.

Some successful teachers taught by giving a series of short presentations using many examples. The examples provided concrete learning and elaboration that were useful for processing new material.

Teaching in small steps requires time and the more-effective teachers spent more time presenting new material and guiding student practice than did the less-effective teachers. In a study of mathematics instruction, the most-effective mathematics teachers spent about twenty-three minutes of a forty-minute period in lecture, demonstration, questioning and working examples. In contrast, the least-effective teachers only spent eleven minutes presenting new material. The more-effective teachers used this extra time to provide additional explanations, give many examples, check for student understanding and provide sufficient instruction so that the students could learn to work independently and not have difficulty. In one study, the least-effective teachers only asked nine questions in a forty-minute period. Compared to the successful teachers, the less-effective teachers gave much shorter presentations and explanations and then they would pass out worksheets and tell students to solve the problems. Under these conditions, the success rate for their students was lower than the success rate that the more-successful teachers obtained in their classrooms. The less-successful teachers were then observed going from student to student and having to explain the material again.

When students were taught a strategy for summarizing a paragraph, the teacher taught the strategy using small steps. First, the teacher modelled and thought aloud as he/she identified the topic of a paragraph. Then, he/she led practice on identifying the topic of new paragraphs. Then, he/she taught students to identify the main idea of a paragraph. The teacher modelled this step and then supervised the students as they practised both finding the topic and locating the main idea. Following this, the teacher taught the students to identify the supporting details in a paragraph. The teacher modelled and thought aloud, and then the students practised. Finally, the students practised carrying out all three steps of this strategy. Thus, the strategy of summarizing a paragraph was divided into smaller steps, and there was modelling and practice at each step.

Suggested readings: Evertson et al., 1980; Brophy & Good, 1990.

3. Ask questions

Questions help students practise new information and connect new material to their prior learning.

Research findings

Students need to practise new material. The teacher's questions and student discussion are a major way of providing this necessary practice. The most successful teachers in these studies spent more than half the class time lecturing, demonstrating and asking questions.

Questions allow a teacher to determine how well the material has been learned and whether there is a need for additional instruction. The most-effective teachers also ask students to explain the process they used to answer the question, to explain how the answer was found. Less-successful teachers ask fewer questions and almost no process questions.

In the classroom

Good and Grouws (1979) conducted an experimental study where the teachers were taught to follow the presentation of new material with a high frequency of questions. Teachers were taught to increase the number of questions and process questions they asked during this guided practice. The teachers in the experimental group increased the number of factual and process questions they asked and the students of teachers in these classes achieved higher scores on the post-test in mathematics than did students of teachers in the control groups.

Imaginative teachers have found ways to involve all students in answering questions. Examples include having each student:

1. Tell the answer to a neighbour.

2. Summarize the main idea in one or two sentences, writing the summary on a piece of paper and sharing this with a neighbour, or repeating the procedures to a neighbour.

3. Write the answer on a card that he or she then holds up.

4. Raise their hand if they know the answer (thereby allowing the teacher to check the entire class).

5. Raise their hand if they agree with the answer that someone else has given.

The purpose of all these procedures (cards, raising hands, writing answers) was to provide active participation for the students and also to allow the teacher to see how many students were correct and confident. The teacher may then re-teach some material when it was considered necessary. An alternative was for students to write their answers and then trade papers with each other.

Other teachers used choral responses to provide sufficient practice when teaching new vocabulary or lists of items. This made the practice seem more like a game. To be effective, however, all students needed to start together, on a signal. When students did not start together, then only the faster students answered.

In addition to asking questions, the more-effective teachers facilitated their students' rehearsal by providing explanations, by giving more examples and by supervising students as they practised the new material.

King (1994) developed a series of stems for questions (see below) that teachers might ask when teaching literature, social science content and science content to their students. Teachers would develop questions based on these stems. Sometimes students would also develop questions from these stems and ask questions of each other.

EXAMPLES OF STEMS FOR QUESTIONS

How are _____ and _____ alike?

What is the main idea of _____?

What are the strengths and weakness of _____?

In what way is _____ related to _____?

Compare _____ and _____ with regard to

_____.

What do you think causes _____?

How does _____ tie in with what we have learned before?

Which one is the best _____ and why?

What are some possible solutions for the problem of _____?

Do you agree or disagree with this statement: _____?

What do you still not understand about _____?

Suggested readings: Good & Grouws, 1979; King, 1994.

4. Provide models

Providing students with models and worked examples can help students learn to solve problems faster.

Research findings

Students need cognitive support to help them learn to solve problems. Modelling and the teacher thinking aloud as he/she demonstrates how to solve a problem are examples of cognitive support.

Worked-out examples are another form of modelling that has been developed by researchers in Australia. Worked-out examples allow students to focus on the specific steps that can solve the problems and thus reduce the cognitive load on their working memory. Modelling and worked examples are used successfully to help students learn to solve problems in mathematics, science, writing and reading comprehension.

In the classroom

Many of the skills that are taught in classrooms can be conveyed by providing prompts, modelling the use of the prompt by the teacher, and then guiding students as they develop independence. When teaching reading comprehension, for example, teachers provided students with prompts that the students could use to ask themselves questions about a short passage. The first step is to give the students prompts that they can use to begin a question. Students were given words such as "who", "where", "why" and "how" to help them begin a question. Then everyone read a passage and the teacher modelled how to use these words to ask a question. Many examples were given.

Then, during guided practice, the teacher helped the students practise asking questions by helping them select a prompt and develop a question that begins with that prompt. The students practised this step many times with lots of support from the teacher.

Then the students read new passages and practised asking questions on their own, with support from the teacher when needed. Finally, students are given short passages followed by questions and the teacher expressed an opinion about the quality of the students' questions.

This same procedure—providing a prompt, modelling, guiding practice and supervising independent practice—can be used for many tasks. When teaching students to write an essay, for example, first the teacher modelled how to write each paragraph, then the students and teacher worked together on two or more new essays and, finally, students worked on their own with supervision from the teacher.

"Worked-out examples" is another form of modelling that has been used to help students learn how to solve problems in mathematics and science. A worked-out example is a step-by-step demonstration of how to perform a task or how to solve a problem. The presentation of workedout examples begins with the teacher modelling and explaining the steps than can be taken to solve a specific problem. The teacher also identifies and explains the underlying principle for these steps.

Usually students are then given a series of problems to complete at their desks as independent practice (sometimes called "seatwork"). But, in the research carried out in Australia, students were given a mixture of regular problems and worked-out examples. Worked-out examples were problems where all the steps were completed for the students. So, during independent practice, students first studied a worked-out example; then they worked-out a regular problem; and then they studied a worked-out example and worked on another problem. In this way, students could use the worked-out examples that showed them how to focus on the essential parts of the problem.

Of course, not all students studied the worked-out examples. To correct this problem, the Australian researchers also presented partiallycompleted problems where only some of the problem was worked out and students had to complete the missing steps. When partiallycompleted problems are presented, students are required to pay more attention to the worked-out example.

Suggested readings: Sweller, 1994; Rosenshine, Chapman & Meister, 1996; Schoenfeld, 1985.

5. Guide student practice

Successful teachers spent more time guiding the students' practice of new material.

Research findings

It is not enough simply to present students with new material, because the material will be forgotten unless there is sufficient rehearsal. An important finding from the information-processing research is that students need to spend additional time rephrasing, elaborating and summarizing the new material in order to store this material in their long-term memory. When there has been sufficient rehearsal, the students are able to retrieve this material easily and, thus, are able to make use of this material to foster new learning and to aid in problem-solving. But when the rehearsal time is too short, students are less able to store or remember or use the material. As we know, it is relatively easy to place something in a filing cabinet, but it can be very difficult to recall where exactly we filed it. Rehearsal helps us remember where we filed it.

A teacher can help this rehearsal process by asking questions, because good questions require the students to process and rehearse the material. Rehearsal is also enhanced when students are asked to summarize the main points, and when they are supervised as they practice new steps in a skill. The quality of storage will be weak if students only skim the material and do not engage in "depth of processing". It is also important that all students process the new material and receive feedback.

In the classroom

In one study the more-successful teachers of mathematics spent more time presenting new material and guiding practice. The more-successful teachers used this extra time to provide additional explanations, to give many examples, to check for student understanding and to provide sufficient instruction so that the students could learn to work independently without difficulty. In contrast, the less-successful teachers gave much shorter presentations and explanations and then they passed out worksheets and told students to work on the problems. Under these conditions, the students made too many errors and had to be re-taught the lesson.

The most-successful teachers presented only small amounts of material at a time. After this short presentation, these teachers then guided student practice. This guidance often consisted of the teacher working the first problems at the blackboard and explaining the reason for each step. This instruction served as a model for the students. This guidance also included asking students to come to the blackboard to work out problems and to discuss their procedures. Through this process, the students seated in the classroom saw additional models.

Although most teachers provided some guided practice, the mostsuccessful teachers spent more time in guided practice, more time asking questions, more time checking for understanding, more time correcting errors and more time having students work out problems with teacher guidance.

Teachers who spent more time in guided practice and had higher success rates also had students who were more engaged during individual work at their desks. This finding suggests that, when teachers provided sufficient instruction during guided practice, the students were better prepared for the independent practice (e.g. seatwork and homework activities) but when the guided practice was too short the students were not prepared for the seatwork and they made more errors during independent practice.

Suggested readings: Evertson et al., 1980; Kirschner, Sweller & Clark, 2006.

6. Check for student understanding

Checking for student understanding at each point can help students learn the material with fewer errors.

Research findings

The more-effective teachers frequently check to see if all the students are learning the new material. This check provides some of the processing that is needed in order to move new learning into the long-term memory. This check also lets teachers know if students are developing misconceptions.

In the classroom

Effective teachers also stopped to check for student understanding. They checked for understanding by asking questions, by asking students to summarize the presentation up to that point or to repeat directions or procedures, or asked students whether they agreed or disagreed with other students' answers. This checking has two purposes: (a) answering the questions might cause the students to elaborate upon the material they learned and augment connections to other learning in their long-term-memory; and (b) checking for understanding can also tell the teacher when parts of the material need to be re-taught.

In contrast, the less-effective teachers simply asked "Are there any questions?" and, if there were no questions, they assumed that the students had learned the material and proceeded to pass worksheets for students to do the work on their own.

Another way to check for understanding is to ask students to think aloud as they worked to solve mathematical problems, to plan an essay or identify the main idea in a paragraph. Another check is to ask students to explain or defend their position to others. Having to explain a position may help students to integrate and elaborate their knowledge in new ways.

Another reason for the importance of teaching in small steps, guiding practice, checking for understanding and obtaining a high success rate comes from the fact that we construct and reconstruct knowledge. We cannot simply repeat what we hear word for word. Rather, we connect our understanding of the new information to our existing concepts or "schema", and we then construct a mental summary: "the gist" of what we have heard. However, when left on their own, many students make errors in the process of constructing this mental summary. These errors occur, particularly, when the information is new and the student does not have adequate or well-formed background knowledge. These constructions are not errors so much as attempts by the students to be logical in an area where their background knowledge is weak. These errors are so common that there is a literature on the development and correction of student misconceptions in science. Providing guided practice after teaching small amounts of new material, and checking for student understanding, can help limit the development of misconceptions.

Suggested readings: Fisher & Frey, 2007; Dunkin, 1978.

7. Obtain a high success rate

It is important for students to achieve a high success rate during classroom instruction.

Research findings

In two of the major studies on the impact of teacher, the investigators found that students in classrooms of the more-effective teachers had a higher success rate as judged by the quality of their oral responses and their individual work. In a study of fourth-grade mathematics, it was found that 82% of students' answers were correct in the classrooms of the most-successful teachers, but the least-successful teachers had a success rate of only 73%. A high success rate during guided practice also leads to a higher success rate when students are working on problems on their own.

The research also suggests that the optimal success rate for student achievement appears to be about 80%. A success rate of 80% shows that students were learning the material, and it also shows that the students were challenged.

In the classroom

The most-effective teachers obtained this success level by "teaching in small steps", that is, by combining short presentations with supervised student practice, and by giving sufficient practice on each part before proceeding to the next step. These teachers frequently checked for understanding and required responses from all students.

It is important that students achieve a high success rate during instruction and on their practice activities. Practice, we are told, makes perfect, but practice can be a disaster if students are practising errors! If the practice does not have a high success level, there is a chance that students are practising and learning errors and once errors have been learned they are very difficult to overcome.

When we learn new material we construct a "gist" of this material in our long-term memory. However, many students make errors in the process of constructing this mental summary. These errors can occur when the information is new and the student did not have adequate or well-formed background knowledge. These constructions were not errors so much as attempts by the students to be logical in an area where their background knowledge was weak. But students were more likely to develop misconceptions if too much material was presented at once, and if teachers did not check for student understanding. Providing guided practice after teaching small amounts of new material, and checking for student understanding, can help limit the development of misconceptions.

I once observed a class where the teacher was going from desk to desk during independent practice and suddenly realized that the students were having difficulty. She stopped the work and told the students not to do these problems for homework and she would re-teach this material the next day. She stopped the work because she did not want the students to practice errors.

Unless all students have mastered the first set of lessons there was a danger that the slower students would fall further behind when the next set of lessons was taught. So there is a need for a high success rate for all students. "Mastery learning" is a form of instruction where lessons are organized into short units and all students are required to master one set of lessons before they proceed to the second set. In mastery learning, tutoring by other students or by teachers was provided to help students master each unit.

Variations of this approach, particularly the tutoring, might be useful in other classroom settings.

Suggested readings: Anderson & Burns, 1987; Frederiksen, 1984.

8. Provide scaffolds for difficult tasks

The teacher provides students with temporary supports and scaffolds to assist them when they learn difficult tasks.

Research findings

Investigators have successfully provided students with scaffolds, or instructional supports, to help them learn difficult tasks. A scaffold is a temporary support that is used to assist a learner. These scaffolds are gradually withdrawn as learners become more competent, although students may continue to rely on scaffolds when they encounter particularly difficult problems. Providing scaffolds is a form of guided practice.

Scaffolds include modelling of the steps by the teacher, or thinking aloud by the teacher as he or she solves the problem. Scaffolds may also be tools, such as cue cards or checklists, that complete part of the task for the students, or a model of the completed task against which students can compare their own work.

The processes of helping students solve difficult problems by modelling and providing scaffolds has been called "cognitive apprenticeship". Students are learning strategies during this apprenticeship that will enable them to become competent readers, writers and problem-solvers. They are aided by a master who models, coaches, provides supports and scaffolds the students as they become independent.

In the classroom

One form of scaffolding is to give students prompts for steps they might use. Prompts such as "who" and "why" and "how" have helped students learn to ask questions while they read. Teaching students to ask questions has been shown to help students' reading comprehension.

Berkowitz (1986) developed a prompt to help students organize material.

1. Draw a central box and write the title of the article in it.

2. Skim the article to find four to six main ideas.

3. Write each main idea in a box below the central box.

4. Find and write two to four important details to list under each main idea.

Another form of scaffolding is thinking aloud by the teacher. For example, teachers might think aloud as they try to summarize a paragraph. They would show the thought processes they go through as they determine the topic of the paragraph and then use the topic to generate a summary sentence. A teacher might think aloud while solving a scientific equation or writing an essay, while providing labels for their processes. Thinking aloud by the teacher provides novice learners with a way to observe "expert thinking" that is usually hidden from the student. Teachers can also study their students' thought processes by asking them to think aloud during their problem-solving processes.

One characteristic of experienced teachers is their ability to anticipate students' errors and warn them about possible errors that some of them are likely to make. For example, a teacher might have students read a passage and then show the class a poorly written topic sentence and ask students to correct this topic sentence. In teaching division or subtraction, students might be shown the places where students frequently made errors and then these errors were discussed.

In some of the studies, students were given a checklist to evaluate their work. One checklist item was: "Have I found the most important information that tells me more about the main idea" or "Does every sentence start with a capital letter". The teacher then modelled use of the checklist.

In some studies, students were provided with expert models to which they could compare their work. For example, when students were taught to generate questions, they could compare their questions with those generated by the teacher. Similarly, when learning to write summaries, students could compare their summaries on a passage with those generated by an expert.

Suggested readings: Pressley et al., 1995; Rosenshine & Meister, 1992.

9. Independent practice

Provide for successful independent practice.

Research findings

In a typical teacher-led classroom, guided practice is followed by independent practice—by students working alone and practising the new material. This independent practice is necessary because a good deal of practice (overlearning) is needed in order to become fluent and automatic in a skill. When material is overlearned it can be recalled automatically, and doesn't take up any space in our working memory. When students become automatic in an area, they can then devote more of their attention to comprehension and application.

Independent practice provides students with the additional review and elaboration they need to become fluent in a skill. This need for fluency applies to facts, concepts and discriminations that must be used in subsequent learning. Fluency is also needed in operations, such as dividing decimals, conjugating a regular verb in a foreign language or completing and balancing a chemical equation.

In the classroom

The more-successful teachers provided for extensive and successful practice, both in the classroom and after class. Independent practice should involve the same material as the guided practice. If guided practice dealt with identifying types of sentences, then independent practice should deal with the same topic or, perhaps, with creating individual compound and complex sentences. It would be inappropriate if this guided practice contained an independent practice assignment that asked students do activities such as: "Write a paragraph using two compound and two complex sentences", because the students have not been adequately prepared for such an activity.

Students need to be prepared for their independent practice. Sometimes, it may be appropriate for a teacher to practice some of the seatwork problems with the entire class before they begin independent practice.

Students were more engaged when their teacher circulated around the room and monitored and supervised their seatwork. The optimal time for these contacts was thirty seconds or less. Classrooms where the teachers had to stop at students' desks and provide a great deal of explanation during seatwork were also classrooms where students were making errors. These errors occurred because the guided practice was not sufficient for students to engage productively in independent practice. This finding suggests the importance of adequately preparing students before they begin their independent practice.

Students helping students

Some investigators (Slavin, 1996) have developed procedures, such as co-operative learning, during which students help each other as they study. Research shows that all students tend to achieve more in these settings than do students in regular settings. Presumably, some of the advantage comes from having to explain the material to someone else and/or having someone else (other than the teacher) explain the material to the student. Co-operative learning offers an opportunity for students to get feedback from their peers about correct as well as incorrect responses, which promotes both engagement and learning. These co-operative/competitive settings are also valuable for helping slower students in a class by providing extra instruction for them in this setting.

Suggested readings: Rosenshine, 2009; Slavin, 1996.

10. Weekly and monthly review

Students need to be involved in extensive practice in order to develop well-connected and automatic knowledge.

Research findings

Students need extensive and broad reading, and extensive practice in order to develop well-connected networks of ideas (schemas) in their long-term memories. When the knowledge on a particular topic is large and well-connected, it becomes easier to learn new information and prior knowledge is more readily available for use. The more one rehearses and reviews information, the stronger these interconnections become. It is also easier to solve new problems when one has a rich, well-connected body of knowledge and strong ties between the connections. One of the goals of education is to help students develop extensive and available background knowledge.

Knowledge that is organized into patterns only occupies a few bits in our limited working memory. So having larger and better connected patterns frees up space in our working memory. This available space can be used for reflecting on new information and for problem-solving. This development of well-connected patterns (also called "unitization" and "chunking") and the freeing of space in the working memory is one of the hallmarks of an expert in a field.

Thus, the research on cognitive processing supports the need for a teacher to assist students by providing for extensive reading of a variety of materials, frequent review, and discussion and application activities. The research on cognitive processing suggests that classroom activities, such as extensive reading of a variety of materials, discussion and frequent review, help students increase the number of pieces of information in their long-term memory and organize this information into patterns and chunks.

The more one rehearses and reviews information, the stronger the interconnections between the materials become. Review also helps students develop their new knowledge into patterns, and helps them acquire the ability to recall past learning automatically.

The best way to become an expert is through practice—thousands of hours of practice. The more the practice, the better the performance.

In the classroom

Some of the successful programmes in elementary schools provided for frequent review. In one successful experimental, study teachers were asked to review the previous week's work every Monday and the previous month's work every fourth Monday. These reviews and tests provided the additional practice that students needed to become skilled, successful performers who could apply their knowledge and skills to new areas.

Many successful programmes provided for extensive review. One way of achieving this goal is to review the previous week's work every Monday and the previous month's work every fourth Monday. Some teachers also gave tests after these reviews. It was also found that even at the secondary level classes that had weekly quizzes scored better on final exams than did classes that had only one or two quizzes during the term. These reviews and tests provide the additional practice that the students need to become skilled, successful performers who can apply their knowledge and skills in new areas.

Teachers face a difficult problem when they are faced with the need to cover a lot of material, but without sufficient review. But the research states (and we know from personal experience) that material that is not adequately practised and reviewed is easily forgotten.

Suggested readings: Good & Grouws, 1979; Kulik & Kulik, 1979.

Conclusion

The ten principles in this pamphlet come from three different sources: (a) research on how the mind acquires and uses information; (b) the instructional procedures that are used by the most successful teachers; and (c) the procedures that were invented by researchers to help students learn difficult tasks. The research from each of these three sources has implications for classroom instruction, and these implications are described in each of these ten principles.

Even though these principles come from three different sources, the instructional procedures that are taken from one source do not conflict with the instructional procedures that are taken from another source. Instead, the ideas from each of the sources overlap and add to each other. This overlap gives us faith that we are developing a valid and research-based understanding of the art of teaching.

References and further reading

Anderson, L.W.; Burns, R.B. (1987). Values, evidence, and mastery learning. *Review of educational research, 57*(2), 215–224, Summer.

Berkowitz, S.J. (1986). Effects of instruction in text organization on sixthgrade students' memory for expository reading. *Reading research quarterly, 21*(2), 161–178.

Brophy, J.E.; Good, T.L. (1986). Teacher behavior and student achievement. In: Wittrock, M.C. (Ed.). *Handbook of research on teaching,* 3rd ed., pp. 328–375. New York, NY: Macmillan.

Brophy, J.; Good, T. (1990). *Educational psychology: a realistic approach.* New York, NY: Longman.

Dunkin, M.J. (1978). Student characteristics, classroom processes, and student achievement. *Journal of educational psychology,* 70(6), 998–1009.

Evertson, C.E. et al. (1980). Relationship between classroom behaviors and student outcomes in junior high mathematics and English classes. *American educational research journal, 17,* 43–60.

Fisher, D.; Frey, A. (2007). *Checking for understanding: formative assessment techniques for your classroom.* Arlington, VA: Association for Supervision and Curriculum Development.

Frederiksen, N. (1984). Implications of cognitive theory for instruction in problem-solving. *Review of educational research, 54*(3), 363–407.

Gage, N.L. (1978). *The scientific basis of the art of teaching.* New York, NY: Teachers College Press.

Good, T.L.; Grouws, D.A. (1979). The Missouri mathematics effectiveness project. *Journal of educational psychology, 71,* 143–155.

Good, T.L.; Grouws, D.A. (1977). Teaching effects: a process-product study in fourth grade mathematics classrooms. *Journal of teacher education,* 28, 40–54.

King, A. (1994). Guiding knowledge construction in the classroom: effects of teaching children how to question and how to explain. *American educational research journal,* 30, 338–368.

Kirschner, P.A.; Sweller, J.; Clark, R.E. (2006). Why minimal guidance during instruction does not work: an analysis of the failure of constructivist, discovery, problem-based, experiential, and inquirybased teaching. *Educational psychologist*, 41, 75–86.

Kulik, J.A.; Kulik, C.C. (1979). College teaching. In: Peterson, P.L.; Walberg, H.J. (Eds.). *Research on teaching: concepts, findings, and implications*. Berkeley, CA: McCutchan.

Laberge, D.; Samuels, S.J. (1974). Toward a theory of automatic information processing in reading. *Cognitive psychology*, 6, 293–323.

Miller, G.A. (1956). The magical number seven, plus or minus two: some limits on our capacity for processing information. *Psychological review*, 1956, 63, 81–97.

Pressley, M. et al. (1995). *Cognitive strategy instruction*, 2nd ed. Cambridge, MA: Brookline Books.

Riley, D. (2019) 'Guided practice', *Dynamite Lesson Plan* [blog]. Available at: www.dynamitelessonplan.com/guided-practice

Rosenshine, B. (2009). The empirical support for direct instruction. In: Tobias, S.; Duffy, T.M. (Eds.). *Constructivist instruction: success or failure?*, ch. 11. New York, NY: Routledge.

Rosenshine, B.; Meister, C. (1992). The use of scaffolds for teaching higherlevel cognitive strategies. *Educational leadership*, April, 26–33.

Rosenshine, B.; Stevens, R. (1986). Teaching functions. In: Witrock, M.C. (Ed.). *Handbook of research on teaching*, 3rd ed., pp. 376–391. New York, NY: Macmillan.

Rosenshine, B.; Chapman, S.; Meister, C. (1996). Teaching students to generate questions: a review of the intervention studies. *Review of educational research*, 66, 181–221.

Schoenfeld, A.H. (1985). *Mathematical problem solving*. New York, NY: Academic Press.

Slavin, R.E. (1996). *Education for all*. Exton, PA: Swets & Zeitlinger.

Stallings, J.A.; Kaskowitz, D. (1974). *Follow through classroom observation*. Menlo Park, CA: SRI International.

Sweller, J. (1994). Cognitive load theory, learning difficulty and instructional design. *Learning and instruction*, 4, 295–312.